Code on Alerts and Indicators, 2009

2010 EDITION

INTERNATIONAL
MARITIME
ORGANIZATION

London, 2010

Published in 2010
by the INTERNATIONAL MARITIME ORGANIZATION
4 Albert Embankment, London SE1 7SR
www.imo.org

Printed in the United Kingdom by CPI Books Limited, Reading RG1 8EX

PEFC
PEFC/06-37-03

ISBN: 978-92-801-1526-0

IMO PUBLICATION
Sales number: IB867E

This publication has been prepared from official documents of IMO, and every effort
has been made to eliminate errors and reproduce the original text(s) faithfully. Readers
should be aware that, in case of inconsistency, the official IMO text will prevail.

018822

Contents

Tables *(continued)*

Foreword

Taking into account changing technology and the continuing evolution of IMO instruments, the Code on Alerts and Indicators, 2009, was developed in accordance with a decision taken by the Maritime Safety Committee (MSC) at its seventy-ninth session. In December 2009, it was adopted by the Assembly at its twenty-sixth session by resolution A.1021(26).

The Code is intended to provide general design guidance and to promote uniformity of type, location and priority for those alerts and indicators required by various IMO instruments and will benefit designers and operators by consolidating in one document the references to priorities, aggregation, grouping, locations and types, including colours and symbols, of shipboard alerts and indicators.

The Code succeeds the Code on Alarms and Indicators, 1995, adopted by resolution A.830(19) in November 1995, which in turn succeeded the Code on Alarms and Indicators adopted by resolution A.686(17) in November 1991.

Resolution A.1021(26)
Adopted on 2 December 2009

CODE ON ALERTS AND INDICATORS, 2009

THE ASSEMBLY,

RECALLING Article 15(j) of the Convention on the International Maritime Organization concerning the functions of the Assembly in relation to regulations and guidelines concerning maritime safety and the prevention and control of marine pollution from ships,

RECALLING ALSO that, by resolution A.830(19), it adopted the Code on Alarms and Indicators, 1995, incorporating therein provisions on alarms and indicators contained in respective IMO instruments,

RECOGNIZING the need to further update the provisions of the Code, thereby ensuring compliance with the requirements of the IMO instruments which have been adopted and/or amended since the Code was adopted and, thus, eliminate contradictions, ambiguities and unnecessary redundancies,

HAVING CONSIDERED the recommendations made by the Maritime Safety Committee at its eighty-sixth session and the Marine Environment Protection Committee at its fifty-ninth session,

1.   ADOPTS the Code on Alerts and Indicators, 2009, set out in the annex to the present resolution;

2.   RECOMMENDS Governments to:

(a)   take appropriate action to implement the Code; and

(b)   use the Code as an international safety standard for designing alarms and indicators for ships, ships' equipment and machinery;

3.   REQUESTS the Maritime Safety Committee and the Marine Environment Protection Committee to keep the Code under review and update it as necessary;

4.   REVOKES resolution A.830(19).

CODE ON ALERTS AND INDICATORS, 2009

1 Purpose and scope

1.1   The Code is intended to provide general design guidance and to promote uniformity of type, location and priority for those alerts and indicators which are required by the International Convention for the Safety of Life at Sea, 1974 (1974 SOLAS Convention), as amended; associated codes (BCH, Diving, FSS, Gas Carrier, 2000 HSC, IBC, IGC, IMDG, LSA, 2009 MODU, and Nuclear Ships Codes); the International Convention for the Prevention of Pollution from Ships, 1973, as modified by the Protocol of 1978 relating thereto (MARPOL), as amended; the Torremolinos Protocol of 1993 relating to the Torremolinos International Convention for the Safety of Fishing Vessels, 1977 (1993 Torremolinos (SFV) Protocol); the Principles of Safe Manning; the Guidelines for inert gas systems (IGS); the Standards for vapour emission control (VEC) systems; the Performance standards for a bridge navigational watch alarm system (BNWAS); and the Revised performance standards for integrated navigation systems (INS).[*]

1.2   The Code will benefit designers and operators by consolidating in one document the references to priorities, aggregation, grouping, locations and types, including colours, symbols, etc., of shipboard alerts and indicators. Where the applicable IMO instruments do not specify the type and location of particular alerts, this information, as far as practicable, is presented in this Code to promote uniform application.

1.3   In order to achieve similar uniformity, the Code also serves as guidance for alerts and indicators included in IMO instruments other than those referred to in 1.1.

1.4   The management and presentation of alerts should conform additionally to the appropriate performance standards adopted by the Organization.

---

[*] See section 11 for a list of instruments to which the Code makes reference.

2   Application

The Code applies to shipboard alerts and indicators.

3   Definitions

3.1   *Alert.* Alerts announce abnormal situations and conditions requiring attention. Alerts are divided into four priorities: emergency alarms, alarms, warnings and cautions.

> **.1**   *Emergency alarm.* An alarm which indicates that immediate danger to human life or to the ship and its machinery exists and that immediate action should be taken.

> **.2**   *Alarm.* An alarm is a high priority of an alert. Condition requiring immediate attention and action, to maintain the safe navigation and operation of the ship.

> **.3**   *Warning.* Condition requiring no immediate attention or action. Warnings are presented for precautionary reasons to bring awareness of changed conditions which are not immediately hazardous, but may become so if no action is taken.

> **.4**   *Caution.* Lowest priority of an alert. Awareness of a condition which does not warrant an alarm or warning condition, but still requires attention out of the ordinary consideration of the situation or of given information.

3.2   The following alerts are classified as emergency alarms:

> **.1**   *General emergency alarm.* An alarm given in the case of an emergency to all persons on board summoning passengers and crew to assembly stations.

> **.2**   *Fire alarm.* An alarm to summon the crew in the case of fire.

> **.3**   *Water ingress detection main alarm.* An alarm given when the water level reaches the main alarm level in cargo holds or other spaces on bulk carriers or single hold cargo ships.

> **.4**   Those alerts giving warning of immediate personnel hazard, including:

>> **.1**   *Fire-extinguishing pre-discharge alarm.* An alarm warning of the imminent release of fire-extinguishing medium into a space.

    .2   *Power-operated sliding watertight door closing alarm.* An alarm required by SOLAS regulation II-1/13.7.1.6, warning of the closing of a power-operated sliding watertight door.

  .5   For special ships (e.g., high-speed craft), additional alarms may be classified as emergency alarms in addition to the ones defined above.

3.3   The following alerts are classified as alarms:

  .1   *Machinery alarm.* An alarm which indicates a malfunction or other abnormal condition of the machinery and electrical installations.

  .2   *Steering gear alarm.* An alarm which indicates a malfunction or other abnormal condition of the steering gear system, e.g., overload alarm, phase failure alarm, no-voltage alarm and hydraulic oil tank low-level alarm.

  .3   *Control system fault alarm.* An alarm which indicates a failure of an automatic or remote control system, e.g., the navigation bridge propulsion control failure alarm.

  .4   *Bilge alarm.* An alarm which indicates an abnormally high level of bilge water.

  .5   *Water ingress detection pre-alarm.* An alarm given when the water level reaches a lower level in cargo holds or other spaces on bulk carriers or single hold cargo ships.

  .6   *Engineers' alarm.* An alarm to be operated from the engine control room or at the manoeuvring platform, as appropriate, to alert personnel in the engineers' accommodation that assistance is needed in the engine-room.

  .7   *Personnel alarm.* An alarm to confirm the safety of the engineer on duty when alone in the machinery spaces.

  .8   *Bridge navigational watch alarm system (BNWAS).* Second and third stage remote audible alarm as required by resolution MSC.128(75).

  .9   *Fire detection alarm.* An alarm to alert the crew in the onboard safety centre, the continuously manned central control station, the navigation bridge or main fire control station or elsewhere that a fire has been detected.

.10 *Fixed local application fire-extinguishing system activation alarm.* An alarm to alert the crew that the system has been discharged, with indication of the section activated.

.11 Alarms indicating faults in alert management or detection systems or loss of their power supplies.

.12 *Cargo alarm.* An alarm which indicates abnormal conditions originating in cargo, or in systems for the preservation or safety of cargo.

.13 *Gas detection alarm.* An alarm which indicates that gas has been detected.

.14 *Power-operated sliding watertight door fault alarm.* An alarm which indicates low level in hydraulic fluid reservoirs, low gas pressure or loss of stored energy in hydraulic accumulators, and loss of electrical power supply for power-operated sliding watertight doors.

.15 Navigation-related alarms as specified in the Revised performance standards for integrated navigation systems (INS) (resolution MSC.252(83), appendix 5).

.16 For special ships (e.g., high-speed craft), additional alerts may be classified as alarms in addition to the ones defined above.

3.4 *Indicator.* Visual indication giving information about the condition of a system or equipment.

3.5 *Signal.* Audible indication giving information about the condition of a system or equipment.

3.6 *Required alert or indicator.* An alert or indicator required by IMO instruments referred to in 1.1. Any other alerts and indicators are referred to in this Code as non-required alerts or indicators.

3.7 *Call.* The request for contact, assistance and/or action from an individual to another person or group of persons, i.e. the complete procedure of signalling and indicating this request.

3.8 *Silence.* Manual stopping of an audible signal.

3.9 *Acknowledge.* Manual response to the receipt of an alert or call.

3.10 *Aggregation.* Combination of individual alerts to provide one alert (one alert represents many individual alerts), e.g., imminent slowdown or shutdown of the propulsion system alarm at the navigation bridge.

3.11 *Grouping.* A generic term meaning the arrangement of individual alerts on alert panels or individual indicators on indicating panels, e.g., steering gear alerts at the workstation for navigating and manoeuvring on the navigation bridge, or door indicators on a watertight door position indicating panel at the workstation for safety on the navigation bridge.

3.12 *Prioritization/Priority.* The ordering of alerts in terms of their severity, function, sequence, etc.

4　General

4.1　The presentation of alerts and indicators should be clear, distinctive, unambiguous and consistent.

4.2　All required alerts should be indicated by both audible and visual means, except the emergency alarms of 3.2 which should be indicated primarily by a signal. In machinery spaces with high ambient noise levels, signals should be supplemented by indicators, presented in accordance with 6.1. Signals and announcements may also be supplemented by indicators in accommodation spaces.

4.3　Where audible alerts are interrupted by public announcements the visual alert should not be affected.

4.4　A new alert condition should be clearly distinguishable from those existing and acknowledged, e.g., existing and acknowledged alarms and warnings are indicated by a constant light and new (unacknowledged) alarms and warnings are indicated by a flashing light and an audible signal. Audible signals should be stopped when silenced or acknowledged. At control positions or other suitable positions as required, alert systems should clearly distinguish among no alert (normal condition), alert, silenced and acknowledged alert conditions.

4.5　Alerts should be maintained until they are acknowledged and the visual indications of individual alerts should remain until the fault has been corrected. If an alert has been acknowledged and a second fault occurs before the first is rectified, the audible signal and visual indication should be repeated.

4.6　Alerts and acknowledged alerts should be capable of being reset only in case the abnormal condition is rectified.

4.7　The presentation and handling of alarms, warnings and cautions indicated on the navigation bridge should comply with the requirements of module C of resolution MSC.252(83) where applicable to ships with integrated navigation systems (INS) and, where fitted, with the requirements of a bridge alert management system.

4.8   Required alert systems should be continuously powered and should have an automatic change-over to a stand-by power supply in case of loss of normal power supply. Emergency alarms and alarms should be powered from the main source of electrical power and from the emergency sources of electrical power defined by SOLAS regulations II-1/42 or II-1/43 unless other arrangements are permitted by those regulations, as applicable, except that:

.1   the power-operated sliding watertight door closing alarm power sources may be those used to close the doors;

.2   the fire-extinguishing pre-discharge alarm power source may be the medium itself; and

.3   continuously charged, dedicated accumulator batteries of an arrangement, location, and endurance equivalent to that of the emergency source of electrical power may be used instead of the emergency source.

4.9   Required rudder angle indicators and power-operated sliding watertight door position indicators should be powered from the main source of electrical power and should have an automatic change-over to the emergency source of electrical power in case of loss of normal power supply.

4.10   Failure of power supply of required alert and alarm systems should be indicated by an audible and visual alarm or warning.

4.11   Required alert and alarm systems should, as far as is practicable, be designed on the fail-to-safety principle, e.g., a detection circuit fault should cause an audible and visual alarm; see also FSS Code, chapter 9, paragraph 2.5.1.5.

4.12   Provision should be made for functionally testing required alerts and indicators. The Administration should ensure, e.g., by training and drills, that the crew is familiar with all alerts.

4.13   Required alert, alarm and indicator systems should be functionally independent of control systems and equipment, or should achieve equivalent redundancy. Any additional requirements for particular alerts in the IMO instruments applicable to the ship should be complied with.

4.14   Software and data for computerized alert and alarm systems should not be permanently lost or altered as a result of power supply loss or fluctuation. Provision should be made to prevent unintentional or unauthorized alteration of software and data.

4.15   Cables for fire and general emergency alarms and public address systems and their power sources should be of a fire-resistant type where they pass through high fire risk areas, and in addition for passenger ships, main vertical fire zones, other than those which they serve. Systems that are self monitoring, fail-safe or duplicated with cable runs as widely separated as is practicable may be exempted provided that their functionality can be maintained. Equipment and cables for emergency alarms and indicators (e.g., watertight doors' position indicators) should be arranged to minimize risk of total loss of service due to localized fire, collision, flooding or similar damage.

4.16   To the extent considered practicable by the Administration, general emergency alarm, fire alarm and fire-extinguishing pre-discharge alarm should be arranged so that the audible signals can be heard regardless of failure of any one circuit or component.

4.17   Means should be provided to prevent normal operating conditions from causing false alerts, e.g., time delays because of normal transients.

4.18   The number of alerts and indicators which are not required to be presented on the navigation bridge should be minimized.

4.19   The system should be designed so that alerts can be acknowledged and silenced at the authorized control position. All alerts presented on the navigation bridge should be capable of being acknowledged and silenced as required in module C of resolution MSC.252(83) where applicable to ships with integrated navigation systems (INS) and, where fitted, with the requirements of a bridge alert management system.

4.20   In order to facilitate maintenance and reduce risk of fire or harm to personnel, consideration should be given to providing means of isolation of sensors fitted to tanks and piping systems for flammable fluids or fluids at high temperature or pressure (e.g., valves, cocks, pockets for temperature sensors).

5   Audible presentation of alerts and calls

5.1   Required alerts should be clearly audible and distinguishable in all parts of the spaces where they are required. Where a distinct difference between the various audible signals and calls cannot be determined satisfactorily, as in machinery spaces with high ambient noise levels, it is permitted to install common audible signal and call devices supplemented by visual indicators identifying the meaning of the audible signal or call.

5.2   The fire-extinguishing pre-discharge alarm should have a characteristic which can be easily distinguished from any other audible signal or call installed in the space(s) concerned. Audible signals of fire alarm and fire detection alarm should have a characteristic which can be easily distinguished from any other audible signal or call installed in the space(s).

5.3   Audible signals and calls should have characteristics in accordance with section 7.

5.4   In large spaces, more than one audible signal or call device should be installed, in order to avoid shock to persons close to the source of sound and to ensure a uniform sound level over all the space as far as practicable.

5.5   Facilities for adjusting the frequency of audible signal within the prescribed limits may be provided to optimize their performance in the ambient conditions. The adjustment devices should be sealed, to the satisfaction of the Administration, after setting has been completed.

5.6   Arrangements should not be provided to adjust the sound pressure level of required audible signals. Where loudspeakers with built-in volume controls are used, the volume controls should be automatically disabled by the release of the alert signal.

5.7   Administrations may accept electronically-generated signals, provided all applicable requirements herein are complied with.

5.8   Administrations may accept the use of a public address system for the general emergency alarm and the fire alarm provided that:

> **.1**   all requirements for those alerts of the LSA Code, FSS Code and the 1974 SOLAS Convention, as amended, are met;
>
> **.2**   all the relevant requirements for required alerts in this Code are met;
>
> **.3**   the system automatically overrides any other input system when an emergency alarm is required and the system automatically overrides any volume controls provided to give the required output for the emergency mode when an emergency alarm is required;
>
> **.4**   the system is arranged to prevent feedback or other interference; and
>
> **.5**   the system is arranged to minimize the effect of a single failure.

5.9   The general emergency alarm, fire alarm (if not incorporated in the general emergency alarm system), fire-extinguishing pre-discharge alarm and machinery alarm should be so arranged that the failure of the power supply or the signal-generating and amplifying equipment (if any) to one will not affect the performance of the others. Where common audible signals and call devices are installed in accordance with 5.1, arrangements should be provided to minimize the effect of such devices' failure.

5.10   The performance standards and functional requirements of the general emergency alarm are specified in the LSA Code, chapter VII, section 7.2. In addition, the sound pressure level should be in the 1/3-octave band about the fundamental frequency. In no case should the level of an audible signal in a space exceed 120 dB(A).

5.11   With the exception of bells, audible signals should have a signal frequency between 200 Hz and 2,500 Hz.

5.12   For the audible presentation of alerts on the navigation bridge, the requirements of resolution MSC.191(79), MSC/Circ.982, resolution A.694(17) and module C of resolution MSC.252(83) where applicable to ships with integrated navigation systems (INS), and, where fitted, the requirements of a bridge alert management system, should be observed.

5.13   For the audible presentation of navigational alerts on the bridge the sound pressure should be at least 75 dB(A) but not greater than 85 dB(A) at a distance of one metre from the systems. Alternatively, it may be allowed to adjust the sound pressure to at least 10 dB(A) above the ambient noise level, if the ambient sound pressure on the bridge can be determined. The upper noise level should not exceed 85 dB(A).

6   Visual presentation of indicators and calls

6.1   Supplemental visual indicators and calls provided in machinery spaces with high ambient noise levels and in accommodation spaces should:

> **.1**   be clearly visible and distinguishable either directly or by reflection in all parts of the space in which they are required;
>
> **.2**   be of a colour and symbol in accordance with tables 7.1.1 to 7.1.3;
>
> **.3**   flash in accordance with 6.2. Instead of individual flashing lights a single flash or rotating white light in addition to a permanent individual indication may be used for light columns;
>
> **.4**   be of high luminous intensity; and
>
> **.5**   be provided in multiples in large spaces.

6.2   Flashing indicators and calls should be illuminated for at least 50% of the cycle and have a pulse frequency in the range of 0.5 Hz to 1.5 Hz.

6.3   Visual indicators on the navigation bridge should not interfere with night vision. For the visual presentation of alerts on the navigation bridge the requirements of resolution MSC.191(79), module C of resolution MSC.252(83), where applicable to ships with integrated navigation systems (INS), and, where fitted, the requirements of a bridge alert management system, should be observed.

6.4   Indicators should be clearly labelled unless standard visual indicator symbols, such as those in tables 7.1.1 to 7.1.3, are used. These standard visual indicator symbols should be arranged in columns for ready identification from all directions. This applies in particular to the emergency alarms in table 7.1.1. Standard visual indicator symbols may also be used on consoles, indicator panels, or as labels for indicator lights.

6.5   Indicator colours should be in accordance with ISO Standard 2412, as deemed appropriate by the Administration. Indicator colours on navigational equipment should be in accordance with resolution MSC.191(79), paragraph 5.7.

6.6   On mobile offshore drilling units (MODUs), where supplemental visual indicators are installed for general emergency alarms, the colour of these supplemental indicators may be amber, provided they flash with a pulse frequency of at least 4 Hz.

7   Characteristics

The emergency alarms, alarms and call signals listed should have the audible and visual characteristics shown in the tables of this section. All other alerts, indicators and call signals should be clearly distinct from those listed in this section, to the satisfaction of the Administration. These tables are not all-inclusive, and other alerts may be added by the Administration in a manner consistent with this Code.

Table 7.1.1 – *Emergency alarms*
(Note: See table 7.2 for audible signals)

Function	IMO instrument	Audible		Visual		Remarks
		Device	Code	Colour	Symbol*	
General emergency alarm	LSA 7.2.1 SOLAS III/6.4 SOLAS II-2/7.9.4	Whistle Siren Bell Klaxon Horn	1.a, 1.b	Green/ White	passengers	Used for summoning passengers to the assembly stations.
					crew	Used for summoning the crew to the boat stations.
						Sound levels in accordance with LSA Code 7.2.1.2, 7.2.1.3
Fire alarm	SOLAS II-2/7.9.4	Bell Klaxon Siren Horn	2, 1.b	Red		Used for summoning the crew to the fire stations on passenger ships.
	FSS 9.2.5.1	Bell Klaxon Siren Horn	2, 3.c, 3.d	Red		Horn/bell in machinery space, buzzer/bell elsewhere.
Fire-extinguishing pre-discharge alarm	FSS 5.2.1.3	Siren Horn	2	Red	**CO₂**	Signal precedes release. Audible signal distinct from all others. When other fire-extinguishing mediums are used they should be clearly identifiable.
Power-operated sliding watertight door closing alarm	SOLAS II-1/13.7.1.6 and II-1/13.8.2	Horn Klaxon Bell	2	Red Green	No symbol allocated	Signal at door precedes and continues during door closing. At remote position; door open – red indicator, door closed – green indicator. Red indicator on navigation bridge flashes while door closes.
Water ingress detection main alarm	SOLAS XII/12.1, XII/12.2 and II-1/25.3	Bell Buzzer Horn	2	Red		For cargo holds used for water ballast and the ballast tanks, an alarm overriding device may be installed.

*   For use with visual indicator columns (see appendix).

Table 7.1.2 – *Alarms*
(Note: See table 7.2 for audible signals. For the presentation of navigation-related alerts, resolution MSC.191(79) should be observed.)

Function	IMO instrument	Audible		Visual*		Remarks
		Device	Code	Colour	Symbol*	
Machinery alarm	SOLAS II-1/51.1	Horn Buzzer	3	Amber		Horn in machinery space, buzzer elsewhere.
Steering gear alarm	SOLAS II-1/29.5.2 II-1/29.8.4 II-1/29.12.2 II-1/30.3	Horn Buzzer	3	Amber		Horn in machinery space, buzzer elsewhere.
Control system fault alarm	SOLAS II-1/29.8.4 II-1/49.5	Horn Buzzer	3	Amber	No symbol allocated	Horn in machinery space, buzzer elsewhere.
Bilge alarm	SOLAS II-1/48	Horn Buzzer	3	Amber		Horn in machinery space, buzzer elsewhere.
Engineers' alarm	SOLAS II-1/38	Horn Buzzer	3	Amber		Horn/buzzer in engineers' corridors, buzzer in engineers' cabins.
Personnel alarm	Present Code 3.3.7, 8.1	Horn Buzzer	3	Amber		Horn in machinery space, buzzer elsewhere.
Fire detection alarm	FSS 8.2.5.2	Bell Buzzer Horn	2	Red		Should automatically actuate fire alarm if not acknowledged in two minutes or less. Horn/ bell in machinery space, buzzer/bell elsewhere.
	SOLAS II-2/7.4.2 FSS 9.2.5.1	Ditto	2	Red		
	FSS 10.2.4.1.3	Ditto	2	Red		

Table 7.1.2 – *Alarms* (continued)

Function		IMO instrument	Audible		Visual*		Remarks
			Device	Code	Colour	Symbol*	
Fixed local application fire-extinguishing system activation alarm		SOLAS II-2/10.5.6.4	Ditto	2	Red		
Water ingress detection pre-alarm		SOLAS XII/12.1, XII/12.2 and II-1/25.3	Bell Buzzer Horn	2	Amber		For cargo holds used for water ballast, an alarm overriding device may be installed.
Alarm system fault alarm		SOLAS II-1/51.2.2	Horn Buzzer	3	Amber	No symbol allocated	Horn in machinery space, buzzer elsewhere.
Flashing light/ Rotating light		6.1 of the present Code	-	-	White	No symbol allocated	
Cargo alarm		IBC, BCH, IGC, Gas Carrier (GC)	Horn Buzzer	3	Amber	No symbol allocated	See tables 9.1.1 to 9.1.3 of the present Code for IMO instrument references. Horn in machinery space, buzzer in engine control room, cargo control station and navigation bridge.
Gas detection alarm	For chlorine gas	IGC 17.14.4.3 17.14.1.4 GC 17.12.5(d)(iii) 17.12.5(a)(iv)	Siren Horn Bell	2	Red	**GAS Cl**	
	Except for chlorine gas	IGC 13.6, 17.9, 16.3.1.2, 16.3.10 GC 13.6, 17.11, 16.2(b), 16.10	Buzzer Horn	3	Amber	**GAS xxx**	xxx Gas abbreviation may be indicated.
Power-operated sliding watertight door fault alarm		SOLAS II-1/13.7.3 II-1/13.7.8	Horn Buzzer	3	Amber	No symbol allocated	Horn in machinery space, buzzer elsewhere.

* For use with visual indicator columns (see appendix).

15

Table 7.1.3 – *Call signals*
(Note: See table 7.2 for audible signals.)

Function	IMO instrument	Audible		Visual*		Remarks
		Device	Code	Colour	Symbol*	
Telephone	SOLAS II-1/50	Horn Buzzer Bell	3.a	White	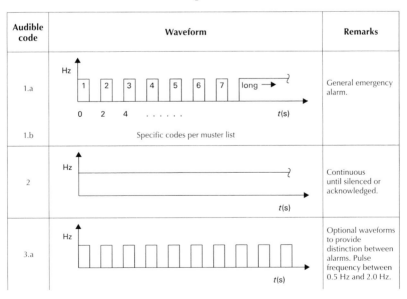	Horn/bell in machinery spaces and engineers' accommodation corridors; buzzer/ bell in engine control room, on navigation bridge and in engineers' cabins.
Engine-room telegraph	SOLAS II-1/37	Horn Bell Buzzer	2, 3.a	White		Horn/bell in machinery space, buzzer/bell in engine control room and on navigation bridge.

* For use with visual indicator columns (see appendix).

Table 7.2 – *Audible signals and call waveforms*

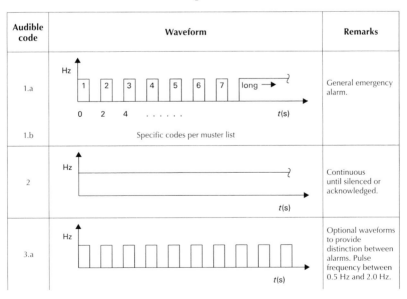

Audible code	Waveform	Remarks
1.a	Hz 1 2 3 4 5 6 7 long → 0 2 4 . . . . . . *t*(s)	General emergency alarm.
1.b	Specific codes per muster list	
2	Hz *t*(s)	Continuous until silenced or acknowledged.
3.a	Hz *t*(s)	Optional waveforms to provide distinction between alarms. Pulse frequency between 0.5 Hz and 2.0 Hz.

Table 7.2 – *Audible signals and call waveforms* (continued)

Audible code	Waveform	Remarks
3.b	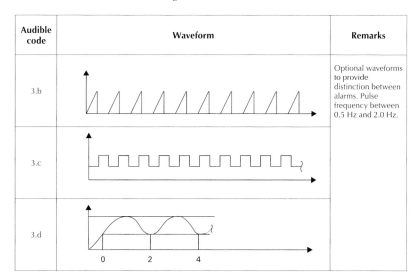	Optional waveforms to provide distinction between alarms. Pulse frequency between 0.5 Hz and 2.0 Hz.
3.c		
3.d		

8 Requirements for particular alarms

8.1 Personnel alarm

8.1.1 The personnel alarm should automatically set off an alarm on the navigation bridge or in the officers' quarters, as appropriate, and, if it is not reset from the machinery spaces in a period satisfactory to the Administration, this should be in a period not exceeding 30 min.

8.1.2 A pre-warning signal should be provided in the machinery spaces which operates 3 min before the alarm required by 8.1.1 is given.

8.1.3 The alarm system should be put into operation:

.1 automatically when the engineer on duty has to attend machinery spaces in case of a machinery alarm; or

.2 manually by the engineer on duty when attending machinery spaces on routine checks.

8.1.4 The alarm system should be disconnected by the engineer on duty after leaving the machinery spaces. When the system is brought into operation in accordance with 8.1.3.1, disconnection should not be possible before the engineer has acknowledged the alarm in the machinery spaces.

8.1.5   The personnel alarm may also operate the engineers' alarm.

8.2   Bridge navigational watch alarm systems (BNWAS)

BNWAS should conform to resolution MSC.128(75) on Performance standards for a bridge navigational watch alarm system.

8.3   Engineers' alarm

In addition to manual operation from the machinery space, the engineers' alarm on ships with periodically unattended machinery spaces should operate when the machinery alarm is not acknowledged in the machinery spaces or control room in a specified limited period of time, depending on the size of the ship but not exceeding 5 min.

8.4   General emergency alarm

8.4.1   Performance standards and functional requirements are provided in the LSA Code, chapter VII, section 7.2. The general emergency alarm system should be capable of being operated from the navigation bridge and at least one other strategic point. For passenger ships there should be an additional activation point in the safety centre. Strategic points are taken to mean those locations, other than the navigation bridge, from where emergency situations are intended to be controlled and the general alarm system can be activated. A fire control station or a cargo control station should normally be regarded as strategic points.

8.4.2   The system should be audible throughout all the accommodation and normal crew working spaces. Normal crew working spaces include spaces where routine maintenance tasks or local control of machinery is undertaken.

8.4.3   In addition, on passenger ships, the system should be recognizable at all places accessible to passengers as well as on all open decks.

9   Grouping and aggregation of alerts and indicators

9.1   Grouping and aggregation should not conceal necessary information from the personnel responsible for the safe operation of the ship.

9.2   Where audible and visual alerts and indicators are required at central positions, e.g., on the navigation bridge, in the machinery space or engine control room, the alerts and indicators, except emergency alarms, should be arranged in groups, as far as is practicable.

9.3   The scope of alerts and indicators will vary with the type of ship and machinery. The basic recommendations given in tables 9.1 to 9.3 should be adhered to.

9.4   Where visual alerts are grouped or aggregated in accordance with 3.10 and 3.11, individual visual alerts should be provided at the appropriate position to identify the specific alert condition.

9.5   The purpose of grouping and aggregation is to achieve the following:

    .1   In general, to reduce the variety in type and number of alerts and indicators so as to provide quick and unambiguous information to the personnel responsible for the safe operation of the ship.

    .2   On the navigation bridge:

        .1   to enable the officer on watch to devote full attention to the safe navigation of the ship;

        .2   to readily identify any condition or abnormal situation requiring action to maintain the safe navigation of the ship; and

        .3   to avoid distraction by alerts which require attention but have no direct influence on the safe navigation of the ship and which do not require immediate action to restore or maintain the safe navigation of the ship.

    .3   In the machinery space/engine control room and at any machinery control station, to readily identify and locate any area of abnormal conditions (e.g., main propulsion machinery, steering gear, bilge level) and to enable the degree of urgency of remedial action to be assessed.

    .4   In the engineers' public rooms and in each of the engineers' cabins on ships where the machinery space/engine control room is periodically unattended, to inform the engineer officer on watch of any alert situation which requires an immediate presence in the machinery space/engine control room.

Table 9.1 – *Grouping/aggregation of alerts and indicators:
machinery space attended, remote control of the main propulsion machinery
from the navigation bridge not provided*

Navigation bridge[*]		Machinery space
One common audible alert device, except emergency alarms (e.g., buzzer, continuous)		Audible alert devices, in accordance with sections 5, 7 and 9
1	2	3
Workstation for navigating and manoeuvring on navigation bridge	Other locations on navigation bridge	Machinery space or control room/station
Individual visual alerts and indicators for: Each required steering gear: - Power unit power failure - Control system power failure - Hydraulic fluid level alarm - Running indication - Alarm system failure alarm Engine-room telegraph Rudder angle indicator Propeller speed/direction/pitch Telephone call	Visual alerts and indicators at any position on the navigation bridge other than the workstation for navigating and manoeuvring for: Required alerts and indicators, as indicated under "Notes" in table 10.1.1 Any non-required alert or indicator which the Administration considers necessary for the officer on watch Fire detection alarm	Visual alerts and indicators grouped at a position in the machinery space or, in the case of ships provided with a control room, in that control room. In complex machinery alarm arrangements, due account should be taken of 9.5.3 Alerts and indicators as indicated under "Notes" in table 10.1.2 Engine-room telegraph

[*] And/or *ship safety centre* on passenger ships.

Table 9.2 – *Grouping/aggregation of alerts and indicators:
machinery space attended, remote control of the main propulsion machinery
from the navigation bridge provided*

Navigation bridge[*]		Machinery space
One common audible alert device, except emergency alarms (e.g., buzzer, continuous)		Audible alert devices, in accordance with sections 3, 5 and 7
1	2	3
Workstation for navigating and manoeuvring on navigation bridge	Other locations on navigation bridge	Machinery space or control room/station
Individual visual alerts and indicators as in column 1 of table 9.1, plus: Failure of remote control for main propulsion machinery Starting air low pressure, when the engine can be started from the navigation bridge Propulsion control station in control	Visual alerts and indicators at any position on the navigation bridge other than the workstation for navigating and manoeuvring as in column 2 of table 9.1, plus: Machinery alarm, if provided	Visual alerts and indicators as in column 3 of table 9.1, plus: Failure of remote control for main propulsion machinery Starting air low pressure Propulsion control station in control Indication of propulsion machinery orders from navigation bridge Alerts and indicators as indicated under "Notes" in table 10.1.2

[*] And/or *ship safety centre* on passenger ships.

Table 9.3 – *Grouping/aggregation of alerts and indicators: machinery space unattended, remote control of the main propulsion machinery from the navigation bridge provided*

Navigation bridge*		Machinery space	Accommodation
One common audible alert device, except emergency alarms (e.g., buzzer, continuous)		Audible alert devices, in accordance with sections 3, 5 and 7	
1	2	3	4
Workstation for navigating and manoeuvring on navigation bridge	Other locations on navigation bridge	Machinery space or control room	Engineers' public spaces and accommodations
Individual visual alerts and indicators as in column 1 of tables 9.1 and 9.2, plus: Override of automatic propulsion shutdown, if provided	Visual alerts and indicators at any position on the navigation bridge other than the workstation for navigating and manoeuvring as in column 2 of tables 9.1 and 9.2, plus: Machinery space fire detection alarm Alarm conditions requiring action by, or the attention of, the officer on watch on the navigation bridge Alerts and indicators as indicated under "Notes" in table 10.1.1	As in column 3 of tables 9.1 and 9.2, plus: Alerts and indicators as indicated under "Notes" in table 10.1.2 Alert system power failure alarm	Engineers' alarm Machinery space fire detection alarm Machinery alarm[†] Steering gear alarm (common)[†] Machinery space bilge alarm[†] Alarm system power failure alarm Alerts and indicators under "Notes" in table 10.1.5

* And/or *ship safety centre* on passenger ships.

† Alarm may be common.

10 Alert and indicator locations

10.1 Required alert and indicator type and location should be in accordance with tables 10.1.1 to 10.1.9.

10.2 Applicable regulations in the IMO instruments referred to should be consulted for additional requirements.

Notes to be applied to tables 10.1.1 to 10.1.9:

(1)   Abbreviation for priorities and indicators:

EM	–	emergency alarm
A	–	alarm
W	–	warning
C	–	caution
I	–	indication/indicator

Abbreviation for presentation:

AU	–	audible alert display (visual may be necessary in high-noise areas)
V	–	visual alert display
AU, V	–	both audible and visual alert display
VI	–	visual indicator
MI	–	measuring indicator

(2)   *Cargo control station* means a position from which the cargo pumps and valves can be controlled. If a central cargo control station is not provided, then the alert or indicator should be located in a suitable position for the operator (such as at the equipment monitored).

(3)   If a cargo control station is not provided, the alert or indication should be given at the gas detector device readout location.

(4)   Where the types of alerts are not specifically identified in the IMO instruments referred to, the recommendations of the IMO Sub-Committee on Bulk Liquids and Gases are enclosed in parentheses, e.g. (A,V).

Table 10.1.1 – *Location: navigation bridge*

IMO instrument	Function	Priority	Display	Notes
SOLAS II-1				
29.11	Rudder angle indicator	I	MI	Column 1, table 9.1
29.5.2	Steering gear power unit power failure	A	AU, V	Ditto
29.8.4	Steering gear control system power failure	A	AU, V	Ditto
29.12.2	Low steering gear hydraulic fluid level	A	AU, V	Ditto
30.1	Steering gear running	I	VI	Ditto
30.3	Steering gear system electric phase failure/overload	A	AU, V	Column 1, table 9.3
31.2.7, 49.5	Propulsion machinery remote control failure	A	AU, V	Column 1, table 9.2, 9.3
31.2.9, 49.7	Low propulsion starting air pressure	A	AU, V	Ditto
31.2.10[†]	Imminent slowdown or shutdown of propulsion system	A	AU, V	Column 1, table 9.2
52	Automatic propulsion shutdown override	I	VI	Column 1, table 9.3

Table 10.1.1 – *Location: navigation bridge* (continued)

IMO instrument	Function	Priority	Display	Notes
SOLAS II-1 **(continued)**				
52	Automatic shutdown of propulsion machinery	A	AU, V	Ditto
51.1.3	Fault requiring action by or attention of the officer on watch	A	AU, V	Column 1, table 9.3 (machinery alarm including 53.4.2 and 53.4.3)
31.2.8	Propeller speed/direction/pitch	I	MI	Column 1, table 9.2
49.6	Propeller speed/direction/pitch	I	MI	Column 1, table 9.3
37	Engine-room telegraph	I	VI	Ditto
13.6 13.8.2, 16.2 13-1.2, 13-1.3, 14.2,15-1.2	Watertight door position	I	VI	Column 2, table 9.1
13.7.3.1	Watertight door low hydraulic fluid level	A	AU, V	Ditto
13.7.3.1 13.7.3.2	Watertight door low gas pressure, loss of stored energy	A	AU, V	Ditto
13.7.8	Watertight door electrical power loss	A	AU, V	Ditto
35-1.2.6.2	High water level alarm	A	AU	!, where required
17-1.1.2, 17-1.1.3	Opening indicator	A	AU, V, VI	Column 2, table 9.1
17-1.2	Shell door position indicator	I	VI	Column 2, table 9.1. Passenger ships with ro–ro cargo spaces or special category spaces. Recommended colours: red – door is not fully closed or not secured, green – door is fully closed and secured
17-1.3	Water leakage detection indicator	I	VI	Column 2, table 9.1. Passenger ships with ro–ro cargo spaces or special category spaces. For details see regulation 17-1.3
25.4	Water level pre-alarm	A	AU, V	Column 2, table 9.1. Bulk carriers and single hold cargo ships other than bulk carriers. For details see resolution MSC.188(79)
25.4	Water level main alarm	EM	AU, V	Ditto
31.2.5, 49.3	Propulsion control station in control	I	VI	Column 1, table 9.2
51.2.2	Alarm system normal power supply failure	A	AU, V	Column 2, table 9.3

Table 10.1.1 – *Location: navigation bridge* (continued)

IMO instrument	Function	Priority	Display	Notes
SOLAS II-2				
4.5.10.1.3	Hydrocarbon gas detection in tanker cargo pump-rooms	A	AU, V	Column 2, table 9.1
7.4.1, 7.4.2	Fire detection in periodically unattended, automated or remotely controlled machinery space	A	AU, V	Column 2, table 9.2
20.3.1.3	Loss of required ventilation	A	AU, V	Column 2, table 9.1
9.6.4	Fire door position	I	VI	Ditto
10.5.6.4	Fixed local application fire-extinguishing system activation	A	AU, V, VI	Column 2, table 9.1. Indication of the activated zone
SOLAS XII				
12.2	Water level pre-alarm	A	AU, V	Column 2, table 9.1. Bulk carriers and single hold cargo ships other than bulk carriers. For details see resolution MSC.188(79)
12.2	Water level main alarm	EM	AU, V	Ditto
Present Code				
3.3.7, 8.1	Personnel alarm	A	AU, V	Column 2, table 9.1
Resolution MSC.128(75), annex				
4.1.2.2, 5.2.2	End of BNWAS dormant period	I	VI	Visible from all operational positions on the bridge where the Officer of the Watch may reasonably be expected to be stationed
4.1.2.3, 5.2.3	BNWAS first stage audible alarm	A	AU	Tone/modulation characteristics and volume level should be adjustable during the commissioning
4.4.1	Malfunction of, or power supply failure to, the BNWAS	W	AU, V	
SOLAS III				
16.9	Position of stabilizer wings	I	VI	Column 2, table 9.1
SOLAS V				
19.2.5.4	Rudder angle, propeller revolutions, the force and direction of thrust and, if applicable, the force and direction of lateral thrust and the pitch and operational mode	I	MI	Column 1, table 9.1

Table 10.1.1 – *Location: navigation bridge* (continued)

IMO instrument	Function	Priority	Display	Notes
Gas or chemical codes				Column 2, table 9.1 for the following:
IBC 15.2.4 BCH 4.19.4	High and low temperature of cargo and high temperature of heat-exchanging medium	A	AU, V	Ammonium nitrate solution
IBC 15.5.1.6 BCH 4.20.6	High temperature in tanks	A	AU, V, MI	Hydrogen peroxide solution over 60% but not over 70%
IBC 15.5.1.7 BCH 4.20.7	Oxygen concentration in void spaces	A	AU, V, MI	Hydrogen peroxide solution over 60% but not over 70%
IBC 15.8.23.1 BCH 4.7.15(a)	Malfunctioning of temperature controls of cooling systems	A	(AU, V)	!, Propylene oxide
IGC 13.4.1 GC 13.4.1	High and low pressure in cargo tank	A	AU, V	High and low pressure alarms
IGC 13.6.4, 17.9 GC 13.6.4, 17.11	Gas detection equipment	A	AU, V	
IGC 13.5.2 GC 13.5.2	Hull or insulation temperature	A	AU, (V), MI	!
IGC 17.18.4.4 GC 17.12.2(d)(iv)	Cargo high pressure, or high temperature at discharge of compressors	A	AU, V	Methylacetylene-propadiene mixtures
IGC 17.14.4.3 GC 17.12.5(d)(iii)	Gas detecting system monitoring chlorine concentration	A	AU, V	!
IGC 17.14.4.4 GC 17.12.5(d)(iv)	High pressure in chlorine cargo tank	A	AU, (V)	!
IBC 15.5.2.5 BCH 4.20.19	High temperature in tanks	A	AU, V, MI	Hydrogen peroxide solution over 8% but not over 60%
IBC 15.5.2.6 BCH 4.20.20	Oxygen concentration in void spaces	A	AU, V, MI	Ditto
IBC 15.10.2 BCH 4.3.1(b)	Failure of mechanical ventilation of cargo tanks	A	(AU, V)	!, Sulphur (molten)
IGC 5.2.1.7 GC 5.2.5(b)	Liquid cargo in the ventilation system	A	(AU, V)	
IGC 8.4.2.1 GC 8.4.2(a)	Vacuum protection of cargo tanks	A	(AU, V)	!
IGC 9.5.2 GC 9.5.2	Inert gas pressure monitoring	A	(AU, V)	!
IGC 13.6.11 GC 13.6.11	Gas detection equipment	A	AU, V	!
IGC 17.14.1.4 GC 17.12.5(a)(iv)	Gas detection after bursting disc for chlorine	A	(AU, V)	!

Table 10.1.1 – *Location: navigation bridge* (continued)

IMO instrument	Function	Priority	Display	Notes
SFV Protocol 1993 Chapter IV				
4(5), 8(1)(e)(iii)	Machinery failure advance alarm	A	AU, V	Column 1, table 9.3 Column 2, table 9.2
6(2)	Oil-fired steam boiler low water level, air supply failure or flame failure	A	AU, V	!, Column 2, table 9.3 II-1/32.2* (see table 7.1.2 of the present Code)
8(1)(d)	Propulsion control station in control	I		Column 1, table 9.2 II-1/31.2.5; II-1/49.3*
8(1)(e)(i), 8(1)(e)(ii)	Propeller speed/direction/pitch	I	MI	Column 1, table 9.2 II-1/31.2.8*
8(1)(g)	Propulsion machinery remote control failure	A	AU, V	Column 1, table 9.2 II-1/31.2.7*
8(1)(h)	Low propulsion starting air pressure	A	AU, V	!, Column 1, table 9.2 II-1/31.2.9*
13(3)	Rudder angle indicator	I	MI	Column 1, table 9.1 II-1/29.11*
13(4)	Steering gear power unit power failure	A	AU, V	Column 1, table 9.1 II-1/29.5.2*
13(5)	Steering gear running	I	VI	Column 1, table 9.1 II-1/30.1*
13(5)	Steering gear overload/no volts	A	AU, V	Column 1, table 9.1 II-1/30.3*
15(5)	Refrigerating machinery spaces alarm	A	AU, V	Column 2, table 9.1
19(1)	High-pressure fuel oil pipe leakage	A	AU, V	!, Column 2, table 9.3
19(3)	Fuel heating high temperature alarm	A	AU, V	!, Column 2, table 9.3
19(5)	Fire detection alarm	A	AU, V	!, Column 2, table 9.3
20(1)	Bilge high water level alarm	A	AU, V	Column 2, table 9.3 II-1/35-1.2.6.2*
22(2)(a)	Essential and important machinery parameters	A	AU, V	Column 2, table 9.3 II-1/51.1.1* (see table 7.1.2 of the present Code)
22(2)(d)	Fault requiring action by or attention of the officer on watch	A	AU, V	Column 1, table 9.3 (machinery alarm including 22(2)(c), 23(2), 23(3)(c) and 23(3)(d)) II-1/51.1.3*
22(3)(b)	Alarm system normal power supply failure	A	AU, V	Column 1, table 9.3 II-1/51.2.2*

Table 10.1.1 – *Location: navigation bridge* (continued)

IMO instrument	Function	Priority	Display	Notes
SFV Protocol 1993 *Chapter IV* **(continued)**				
24	Automatic propulsion shutdown override	I	VI	Column 1, table 9.3 II-1/52*
24	Automatic shutdown of propulsion machinery	A	AU, V	Column 1, table 9.3 II-1/52*
Chapter V				
14(2)(b)	Fire detection or automatic sprinkler operation	A	AU, V	Column 2, table 9.1 II-2/10*
15(2)(b)	Fire detection alarm	A	AU, V	Column 2, table 9.1 II-2/7*
IGS				
3.14.11	Low water level alarm	A	AU, V	
2000 HSC Code				
7.7.1	Automatic smoke detection system in areas of major and moderate fire hazard and other enclosed spaces in accommodation not regularly occupied	I	VI	!, Column 2, table 9.2
7.7.1	Automatic smoke detection and fire detection (with detectors sensing other than smoke) in main propulsion machinery room(s) additionally supervised by TV cameras monitored from the operating compartment	I	VI	Column 2, table 9.2
+7.7.1.2	Fixed fire detection and fire alarm systems' power loss or fault condition	A	AU, V	Column 2, table 9.2
+7.7.1.1.4	Fire detection signal	A	AU	Column 2, table 9.2 at alarm location easily accessible to crew at all time
7.7.1.1.6	Fire detection manually operated call point section unit indicator	A	AU, V	Column 2, table 9.3
7.7.2.1	Fire detection for periodically unattended machinery spaces	A	AU, V	Column 2, table 9.3 II-2/7.4.2*
7.8.1.2	Fire door position	I	VI	Column 2, table 9.2 II-2/9.6.4*
7.8.5.3	Loss of required ventilation	A	AU, V	Column 2, table 9.2 II-2/20.3.1.3*
7.9.3.3.3	Fire door closing	I	VI	!, Column 2, table 9.2 II-2/9.6.4*

Table 10.1.1 – *Location: navigation bridge* (continued)

IMO instrument	Function	Priority	Display	Notes
2000 HSC Code (continued)				
7.13.1	Manually operated sprinkler system alarms	I	I	!, Column 2, table 9.2
7.15	Smoke detection system for cargo spaces	I	VI	!, Column 2, table 9.2
9.1.14	Liquid cooling system failure	A	AU, V	!
9.2.1	Automatic fire detection system	A	AU, V	Column 2, table 9.3 II-2/7.4.1.2; II-2/7.4.2*
9.2.1	Bilge alarm	A	AU, V	Column 2, table 9.3 II-1/48.1; II-1/48.2*
9.2.1	Remote machinery alarm system	A	AU, V	Column 2, table 9.3
9.4.2	Fuel line failure	A	AU, V	Column 2, table 9.2
9.4.5	Lubricating oil pressure or lubricating oil level falling below a safe level	A	AU, V	Column 2, table 9.2
9.5.6	Lubricating fluid supply failure or lubrication fluid pressure loss	A	AU, V	Column 2, table 9.2
10.3.12	Unattended space bilge alarm	A	AU, V	!, Column 2, table 9.2 II-1/48.1*
11.2.1	Failure of any remote or automatic control system	A	AU, V	Column 2, table 9.3
11.4.1	Malfunction or unsafe condition	A	AU, V	!, Column 2, table 9.2
11.4.1.1	Indication of conditions requiring immediate action	EM	AU, V	Column 2, table 9.2; distinctive alarms in full view of crew members
11.4.1.2	Indication of conditions requiring action to prevent degradation to an unsafe condition	C	V	Column 2, table 9.2; visual display to be distinct from that of alarms referred to in 11.4.1.1 of the 2000 HSC Code
12.3.9	Emergency battery discharge	I	VI	Column 2, table 9.2 II-1/42.5.3; II-1/43.5.3*
12.5.1	Steering system electric overload	A	AU, V	!, Column 2, table 9.2 II-1/30.3*
12.5.2	Steering system electric phase failure	A	AU, V	Column 2, table 9.2 II-1/30.3*
12.6.3	Electrical distribution system low insulation level	A or I	AU or VI	!, Column 2, table 9.2 II-1/45.4.2*
13.7	Rudder angle indicator and rate-of-turn indicator	I	VI	Column 2, table 9.2 5.4.3 of the 2000 HSC Code II-1/29.11*, V/19.2.5.4*

Table 10.1.1 – *Location: navigation bridge* (continued)

IMO instrument	Function	Priority	Display	Notes
2000 HSC Code (continued)				
13.11.2	Propulsion indicator	I	VI	Column 2, table 9.2
13.11.3	Emergency steering position compass reading indicator	I	VI	Column 2, table 9.2
2009 MODU Code				
7.4.1	Propeller pitch indicator	I	VI	Column 2, table 9.1
7.4.2.5, 8.5.5	Propulsion station in control indication	I	VI	Columns 1 and 3, table 9.2 II-1/31.2.5; II-1/49.3*
7.4.2.7, 8.5.7	Propulsion machinery remote control failure	A	AU, V	Column 1, table 9.2 II-1/31.2.7; II-1/49.5*
7.4.2.8	Propeller speed/direction/pitch	I	MI	Column 1, table 9.2 II-1/31.2.8*
7.4.2.9, 8.5.9	Low starting air pressure	A	AU, V	Columns 1 and 3, table 9.2 II-1/31.2.9; II-1/49.7*
7.4.2.10	Imminent slowdown or shutdown of the propulsion	A	AU, V	Column 1, table 9.2
7.5.15	Rudder angle indicator	I	MI	Column 1, table 9.1 II-1/29.11*
7.6.1	Steering gear running	I	VI	Columns 1 and !3, table 9.1 II-1/30.1*
7.6.3	Steering gear phase failure/ overload alarm	A	AU, V	Column 1, table 9.3 II-1/30.3*
8.5.8	Propeller speed/direction/pitch	I	MI	Column 1, table 9.3 II-1/49.6*
8.7.1	Fault requiring attention	A	AU, V	Column 1, table 9.3, including 8.3.5.1, 8.4.1, 8.8.5 and 8.9 of the 2009 MODU Code II-1/51.1.3*
8.7.3	Alarm system normal supply failure	A	AU, V	Column 2, table 9.3 II-1/51.2.2*
9.10.1	Fire detection system alarm	A	AU, V	Column 2, table 9.1
9.11.1, 9.12.1	Gas detection and alarm system	A	AU, V	!, Column 2, table 9.1
FSS Code				
+8.2.5.2.1, +9.2.5.1, 9.2.5.1.3	Fire detection or automatic sprinkler operation	A	AU, V	Column 2, table 9.1
+8.2.5.2.1, +9.2.5.1.5, +9.2.5.1	Fire detection system fault	A	AU, V	Ditto

Table 10.1.1 – *Location: navigation bridge* (continued)

IMO instrument	Function	Priority	Display	Notes
FSS Code (continued)				
10.2.4.1.4	Smoke detection system power loss	A	AU, V	Ditto
+10.2.4.1.3, +10.2.2.3	Smoke detection	A !	AU, V, VI	Ditto
15.2.4.2.3.1	Inert gas supply main pressure	!	MI	Ditto; forward of non-return devices
15.2.4.2.3.1	Inert gas pressure	!	MI	Column 2, table 9.1. In slop tanks of combination carriers

*   Cross-reference to SOLAS regulation.

**   Watertight door alarms may be grouped in one common failure alarm for each door provided that individual alarms are available at the watertight door emergency control positions above the bulkhead deck.

†   Refer to II-1/31.6.

!   No location specified in other IMO instruments. Location is recommended.

+   These alarms may be omitted if they are provided at the central fire control station.

Table 10.1.2 – *Location: machinery space/machinery control room*

IMO instrument	Function	Priority	Display	Notes
SOLAS II-1				
29.12.2	Low steering gear fluid level	A	AU, V	Column 3, table 9.1
30.1	Steering gear running	!	VI	Ditto
30.3	Steering system electric phase failure or overload	A	AU, V	Ditto
31.2.7, 49.5	Propulsion machinery remote control failure	A	AU, V	Column 3, tables 9.2 and 9.3
31.2.9, 49.7	Low propulsion starting air pressure	A	AU, V	Ditto
32.2	Oil-fired boiler low water level, air supply failure, or flame failure	A	AU, V	Column 3, table 9.1
32.3	Propulsion boiler high water level	A	AU, V	Ditto
31.2.5, 49.3	Propulsion control station in control	!	VI	Column 3, table 9.2
37	Engine-room telegraph	!	VI	Column 3, table 9.1
31.2.4, 49.2	Propulsion machinery orders from bridge	!	VI	Column 3, table 9.2

Table 10.1.2 – *Location: machinery space/machinery control room* (continued)

IMO instrument	Function	Priority	Display	Notes
SOLAS II-1 *(continued)*				
47.1.1, 47.1.2	Boiler and propulsion machinery internal fire	A	AU, V	Column 3, table 9.3
47.2	Internal combustion engine monitors	I	MI	Ditto
48.1, 48.2	Bilge monitors	A	AU, V	Ditto
51.2.2	Alarm system normal power supply failure	A	AU, V	Ditto
53.4.3, 51.1.1	Essential and important machinery parameters	A	AU, V	Column 3, table 9.3 (machinery alarm)
42.5.3, 43.5.3	Emergency battery discharge	I	VI	Column 3, table 9.1
52	Automatic shutdown of propulsion machinery	A	AU, V	Column 3, table 9.3
52	Automatic propulsion shutdown override	I	VI	Ditto
53.4.2	Automatic change-over of propulsion auxiliaries	A	AU, V	Ditto
45.4.2	Electrical distribution system low insulation level	A or I	AU or I	!, Column 3, table 9.1
SOLAS II-2				
7.4.1, 7.4.2	Fire detection in periodically unattended, automated or remotely controlled machinery space	A	AU, V	Column 3, table 9.2
4.2.2.5.2	High-pressure fuel oil leakage	A	AU, V	Column 3, table 9.3
4.2.5.2	Service fuel oil tank high temperature	A	AU, V	Ditto
4.5.10.1.3	Hydrocarbon gas detection in tankers cargo pump-rooms	A	AU, V	Column 3, table 9.1
10.5.6.4	Fixed local application fire-extinguishing system activation	A I	AU, V, I	Column 3, table 9.1 Indication of the activated zone
Gas or chemical codes				
IGC 16.3.1.1 GC 16.2(a)	Loss of inert gas pressure between pipes	A	AU, V	!, Column 3, table 9.1
IGC 16.3.10 GC 16.10	Cargo gas/fuel system gas detection	A	AU, V	!, Ditto

Table 10.1.2 – *Location: machinery space/machinery control room* (continued)

IMO instrument	Function	Priority	Display	Notes
Gas or chemical codes (continued)				
IGC 16.3.1.2 GC 16.2(b)	Flammable gas in ventilation duct	A	(AU, V)	!, Ditto
IGC 16.3.4 GC 16.5	Flammable gas in ventilation casing	A	(AU, V)	!, Ditto
Present Code				
3.3.7, 8.1	Personnel alarm	A	AU, V	Column 3, table 9.1
SFV Protocol 1993 Chapter IV				
6(2)	Oil-fired steam boiler low water level, air supply failure or flame failure	A	AU, V	!, II-1/32.2*
8(1)(e)(iii)	Machinery failure advance alarm	A	AU, V	!
8(1)(d)	Propulsion control station in control	I	VI	Column 3, table 9.2 II-1/31.2.5; II-1/49.3*
8(1)(g)	Propulsion machinery remote control failure	A	AU, V	!, Column 3, table 9.2 II-1/31.2.7*
8(1)(h)	Low propulsion starting air pressure	A	AU, V	!, Column 3, table 9.2 II-1/31.2.9*
15(4)(b)	Refrigerant leak alarm	A	AU, V	
17(6)	Emergency battery discharge	I	VI	!, Column 3, table 9.1 II-1/42.5.3*
18(4)(b)	Electrical distribution system low insulation level	A	AU or VI	!, Column 3, table 9.1 II-1/45.4.2*
19(7)	Internal combustion engine monitors	I	MI	Column 3, table 9.3 II-1.47.2*
22(2)(a)	Essential and important machinery parameters	A	AU, V	Column 3, table 9.3 II-1/51.1.1*
22(3)(b)	Alarm system normal power supply failure	A	AU, V	Column 3, table 9.3 II-1/51.1.1*
23(2)	Automatic change-over of propulsion auxiliaries	A	AU, V	Column 3, table 9.3 II-1/53.4.2*
24	Automatic shutdown of propulsion machinery	A	AU, V	Column 3, table 9.3 II-1/52*
24	Automatic propulsion shutdown override	I	VI	Column 3, table 9.3 II-1/52*

Table 10.1.2 – *Location: machinery space/machinery control room* (continued)

IMO instrument	Function	Priority	Display	Notes
IGS				
3.14.11	Low water level alarm	A	AU, V	Column 3, table 9.1
MARPOL Annex I				
14.7	Alarm for excessive oil content in oily mixture discharge into the sea	A	(AU, V)	!
2000 HSC Code				
7.7.2	Fire detection signal	A	AU, V	Column 3, table 9.2
7.7.3.1	Fire detection for periodically unattended machinery spaces	A	AU, V	Column 3, table 9.3 II-2/7.4.2*
9.2.1	Automatic fire detection system	A	AU, V	Column 3, table 9.3 II-2/7.4.1.2; II-2/7.4.2*
9.2.1	Bilge alarm	A	AU, V	Column 3, table 9.3 II-1/48.1; II-1/48.2*
9.2.1	Remote machinery alarm system	A	AU, V	Column 3, table 9.3
9.4.2	Fuel line failure	A	AU, V	Column 3, table 9.2
9.4.5	Lubricating oil pressure or lubricating oil level falling below a safe level	A	AU, V	Column 3, table 9.2
9.5.6	Lubricating fluid supply failure or lubrication fluid pressure loss	A	AU, V	Column 3, table 9.2
10.2.7.3	High temperature alarm (oil fuel or settling tank)	A	V	!
10.3.12	Unattended space bilge alarm	A	V	!, Column 3, table 9.2, II-1/48.1*
11.2.1	Failure of any remote or automatic control system	A	AU, V	Column 3, table 9.3
11.4.1	Malfunction or unsafe condition	A	AU, V	Column 3, table 9.2
11.4.1.3	Indication of conditions in 11.4.1.1 requiring immediate action	A	AU, V	
11.4.1.3	Indication of conditions in 11.4.1.2 requiring action to prevent degradation to an unsafe condition	A	AU, V	Column 3, table 9.2; visual display to be distinct from that of alarms referred to in 11.4.1.1 of the 2000 HSC Code
11.5	Shutdown system activation	A	AU, V	!, Column 3, table 9.2

33

Table 10.1.2 – *Location: machinery space/machinery control room* (continued)

IMO instrument	Function	Priority	Display	Notes
2000 HSC Code (continued)				
12.5.1	Steering system electric overload	A	AU, V	!, Column 3, table 9.2 II-1/30.3*
12.5.2	Steering system electric phase failure	A	AU, V	Column 3, table 9.2 II-1/30.3*
12.6.3	Electrical distribution system low insulation level	A or I	AU or VI	!, Column 3, table 9.2 II-1/45.4.2*
2009 MODU Code				
4.3.7	Machinery failure pre-alarm	A	AU, V	!, Column 3, table 9.1
4.6.2	Manual overriding of the automatic control indicator	I	VI	Column 3, table 9.1
5.4.12	Emergency battery discharge	I	VI	Column 3, table 9.1 II-1/42.5.3*
5.6.7	Electrical distribution system low insulation level	A or I	AU or VI	!, Column 3, table 9.1 II-1/45.4.2*
7.3.1	Water tube boiler high water level alarm	A	AU, V	Column 3, table 9.1
7.4.2.4, 8.5.4	Propulsion machinery orders from bridge	I	VI	Column 3, table 9.2 II-1/31.2.4; II-1/49.2*
7.4.2.5, 8.5.5	Propulsion station in control indication	I	VI	Columns 1 and 3, table 9.2 II-1/31.2.5; II-1/49.3*
7.4.2.9	Low starting air pressure	A	AU, V	Columns 1 and 3, table 9.2 II-1/31.2.9*
7.4.2.10	Imminent slowdown or shutdown of the propulsion system	A	AU, V	Column 1, table 9.2
7.6.1	Steering gear running	I	VI	Columns 1 and !3, table 9.1 II-1/30.1*
8.3.1, 4.8.7	High-pressure fuel oil pipe leakage	A	AU, V	!, Column 3, table 9.3 II-2/4.2.2.5.2*
8.3.3	Fuel heating temperature alarm	A	AU, V	!, Column 3, table 9.3 II-2/4.2.5.2*
8.3.6	Fire detection alarm for boiler/propulsion machinery	A	AU, V	!, Column 3, table 9.3 II-1/47.1*
8.3.7	Internal combustion engine monitors	I	MI	Column 3, table 9.3 II-1/47.2*
8.5.7	Propulsion machinery remote control failure	A	AU, V	Column 3, table 9.3 II-1/49.5*

Table 10.1.2 – *Location: machinery space/machinery control room* (continued)

IMO instrument	Function	Priority	Display	Notes
2009 MODU Code *(continued)*				
8.7.1	Fault requiring attention	A	AU, V	At a normally manned control station in addition to main machinery control station including 8.3.5.1, 8.4.1, 8.8.5 and 8.9 of the 2009 MODU Code II-1/51.1*
8.8.2	Automatic change-over of propulsion auxiliaries	A	AU, V	Column 3, table 9.3 II-1/53.4.2*
FSS Code				
15.2.4.3.1	Inert gas system:			Column 3, table 9.1
15.2.4.3.1.1	– low water pressure/flow	A	AU, V	
15.2.4.3.1.2	– high water level	A	AU, V	
15.2.4.3.1.3	– high gas temperature	A	AU, V	
15.2.4.3.1.4	– blower failure	A	AU, V	
15.2.4.3.1.5	– oxygen content	A	AU, V	
15.2.4.3.1.6	– power supply failure	A	AU, V	
15.2.4.3.1.7, 15.2.2.4.6	– water seal low level	A	AU, V	
15.2.4.3.1.8, 15.2.4.3.4	– low gas pressure	A	AU, V	
15.2.4.3.1.9	– high gas pressure	A	AU, V	
15.2.4.3.2	Gas generator failure:			
15.2.4.3.2.1	– low fuel supply	A	AU, V	
15.2.4.3.2.2	– power supply failure	A	AU, V	
15.2.4.3.2.3	– control power failure	A	AU, V	
15.2.4.2.3.2	Inert gas oxygen	I	MI	Ditto

*   Cross-reference to SOLAS regulation.

!   No location specified in other IMO instruments. Location is recommended.

Table 10.1.3 – *Location: central fire control station where provided*

IMO instrument	Function	Priority	Display	Notes
SOLAS II-2				
+7.4.1, 7.4.2	Fire detection in periodically unattended, automated or remotely controlled machinery space	A	AU, V	
SFV Protocol 1993 Chapter V				
14(3)(c)	Automatic sprinkler system pressure	I	MI	
2000 HSC Code				
+7.7.1.1.2	Fixed fire detection and alarm systems' power loss or fault condition	A	AU, V	
+7.7.1.1.4	Fire detection signal	A	AU, V	
2009 MODU Code				
9.10.1	Fire detection system	A I	AU, V VI	
9.11.1, 9.12.1	Gas detection and alarm systems	A	A, V	!
FSS Code				
8.2.4.2.5	Automatic sprinkler system pressure	I	MI	
+8.2.5.2.1, +9.2.5.1.2, 9.2.5.1.3	Fire detection or automatic sprinkler operation	A	AU, V	
+8.2.5.2.1, +9.2.5.1.5, +9.2.5.1.2	Fire detection system fault	A	AU, V	
+10.2.4.1.4	Smoke detection system power loss	A	AU, V	
+10.2.4.1.3, +10.2.2.3	Smoke detection	A I	AU, V VI	

! No location specified in other IMO instruments. Location is recommended.

+ These alarms may be omitted if the central fire control station is on the navigation bridge.

Table 10.1.4 – *Location: at the equipment or at the location being monitored*

IMO instrument	Function	Priority	Display	Notes
SOLAS II-1				
29.11	Rudder angle indicator	I	MI	At the steering gear compartment
15.8.2.1, 15.8.3	Shell valve closure	I	I	
32.6	Water level of essential boiler	I	MI	
13.7.1.6	Watertight door closing	EM	AU	Distinct from other alarms in area; in passenger areas and high-noise areas, add intermittent visual alarm
13.7.3.2	Watertight door loss of stored energy	A	AU, V	At each local operating position
33.3	Steam pressure	I	MI	
SOLAS II-2				
10.9.1.1.1 IBC 11.2.1	Release of fire-extinguishing medium	EM	AU	Cargo pump-room
4.2.2.3.5	Fuel oil tank level	I	MI	If provided
4.2.2.3.5.1.1 4.2.2.3.5.2	Fuel oil tank level	I	MI	
Gas or chemical codes				
IGC 9.5.1 GC 9.5.1	Content of oxygen in inert gas/ trace of oxygen in nitrogen	A	(AU, V) MI	
IGC 3.6.3 GC 3.6.3	Warning on both sides of the airlock	A	AU, V	
IGC 8.2.8.2 GC 8.2.8(b)	Indicates which one of the pressure relief valves is out of service	I	VI	
IGC 11.5 GC 11.5.2	Inerting/extinguishing medium release	EM	AU	Gas-dangerous enclosed spaces
GC 13.4	Cargo pressure	I	MI	Local gauges required by 13.4.1, 13.4.2, 13.4.3 and 13.4.4 of the GC Code
IGC 13.6, 17.9 GC 13.6, 17.11	Gas detection equipment	A	AU, V	
SFV Protocol 1993 *Chapter II*				
13(1)	Shell valve closure	A	AU, V	II-1/15.8.2.1*
13(2)	Shell valve closure	A	AU, V	II-1/15.8.3*
Chapter IV				
11(7)	Collision bulkhead valve closure	I	VI	II-1/35-1.3.12*
13(3)	Rudder angle indicator	I	MI	

Table 10.1.4 – *Location: at the equipment or at the location being monitored* (continued)

IMO instrument	Function	Priority	Display	Notes
SFV Protocol 1993 Chapter IV (continued)				
15(4)(a)	Refrigerant leak indicator	I	VI	
15(5)	Refrigerating machinery spaces alarm	A	AU, V	At escape exits
Chapter V				
14(3)(c)	Automatic sprinkler system pressure	I	MI	At each section stop valve
14(5)(a)	Automatic sprinkler tank level	I	MI	
15(2)(b)	Fire detection alarm	A	AU	To ensure fire alarm sounding on the deck where the fire is detected
IGS				
3.15.3.2.1	Effluent drain valve position indicator	I	VI	!
6.2	Tank pressure sensors	I	MI	!
VEC systems				
2.3.1	Isolation valve position indicator	I	VI	
2.4.1.3	Liquid level indicator	I	MI	At the location where cargo transfer is controlled
2.4.1.4	Liquid level indicator	I	MI	Portable gauging device on the tank
3.2.1.3	Cargo vapour shutoff valve position indicator	I	VI	Near terminal vapour connection
3.3.3	Terminal vapour pressure sensing device	I	MI	!, (3)
3.3.3.2	Terminal vapour pressure alarm	A	AU, V	!, (3)
3.3.3.3	Signal for sequential shutdown of onshore pumps and remotely operated cargo vapour shutoff valve	A	(AU, V)	!, (3)
IMDG Code (Vol. I)				
7.7.3.4	Cargo control temperature less than +25°C	A	AU, V	!, Alarms independent of power supply of the refrigeration system
2000 HSC Code				
7.7.3.3.7	Release of fire-extinguishing medium	EM	AU, V	Spaces in which personnel normally work or to which they have access

Table 10.1.4 – *Location: at the equipment or at the location being monitored* (continued)

IMO instrument	Function	Priority	Display	Notes
2000 HSC Code (continued)				
7.9.3.3.2	Fire door closing	EM	AU	Sounding alarm before the door begins to move and until completely closed
7.13.1	Manually operated sprinkler system alarms	I	M, I	!, Column 2, table 9.2
10.9.5	Bilge cock and valve positions indication	I	VI	To indicate open or closed position
1995 Diving Code				
2.5.3	Diving bell internal pressure	I	MI	!, At the location of the attendant monitoring diving operations
2.5.5	Diving bell, etc., overpressure alarm	A	AU, V	!, At the location of the attendant monitoring diving operations
2.9.3	Diving equipment fire detection alarm	A	AU, V	!, At the location of the attendant monitoring diving operations
2009 MODU Code				
3.6.5.2	Watertight door and hatch cover positions alarm	A	AU, V	
4.4.5	Water level of essential boiler	I	MI	II-1/32.6*
4.5.3	Steam pressure	I	MI	II-1/33.3*
4.9.6	Bilge valve indicator	I	VI	II-1/35-1.3.12*
4.10.8	Ballast valve position indicator	I	VI	
4.12.11	Cable tension, windlass power load and amount of cable paid out	I	VI	
FSS Code				
5.2.1.3.2	Release of fire-extinguishing medium	EM	AU	
8.2.4.2.5	Automatic sprinkler system pressure	I	MI	At each section stop valve
8.2.3.2.1	Automatic sprinkler system tank level	I	MI	
15.2.3.1.1	Flue gas isolating valve open/closed	I	VI	
15.2.4.1	Inert gas discharge temperature/pressure	I	MI	Measured at discharge of gas blower

* Cross-reference to SOLAS regulation.

! No location specified in other IMO instruments. Location is recommended.

(3) See notes following paragraph 10.2.

Table 10.1.5 – *Location: engineers' accommodation*

IMO instrument	Function	Priority	Display	Notes
SOLAS II-1				
38	Engineers' alarm	A	AU	Column 4, table 9.3
51.1.2, 51.1.5	Fault requiring attention of the engineer on duty	A	AU, V	Ditto (machinery alarm)
SOLAS II-2				
7.4.1, 7.4.2	Fire detection in periodically unattended, automated or remotely controlled machinery space	A	AU, V	Ditto
Present Code				
3.3.7, 8.1	Personnel alarm	A	AU, V	Column 4, table 9.3 (when the navigation bridge is unmanned)
SFV Protocol 1993 Chapter IV				
14	Engineers' alarm	A	AU	Column 4, table 9.3 II-1/38*
22(2)(b), 22(2)(c)	Fault requiring attention of engineer on duty	A	AU, V	Column 4, table 9.3 II-1/51.1.2; II-1/51.1.5*
2000 HSC Code				
7.7.2.1	Fire detection for periodically unattended machinery spaces	A	AU, V	Column 4, table 9.3 II-2/7.4.1.1; II-2/7.4.2*
2009 MODU Code				
7.8	Engineers' alarm	A	AU	Column 4, table 9.3 II-1/38*
8.7.1	Fault requiring attention	A	AU	Activate engineers' alarm required by 7.8 including 8.3.5.1, 8.4.1, 8.8.5 and 8.9, all of the 2009 MODU Code II-1/51.1.5*

*   Cross-reference to SOLAS regulation.

Table 10.1.6 – *Location: miscellaneous*

IMO instrument	Function	Priority	Display	Notes
SOLAS II-1				
13.6, 13-1.2, 13-1.3	Watertight door position	I	VI	At operating stations from which the door is not visible. At all remote operating positions
35-1.3.12	Bilge cocks and valves position	I	VI	At their place of operation
SOLAS II-2				
7.4.1, 7.4.2	Fire detection in periodically unattended, automated or remotely controlled machinery space	A	AU, V	Alarm at attended location when navigation bridge is unmanned
7.9.1	Fire detection alarm	A	AU, V	Alarm at location to ensure that any initial fire detection alarm is immediately received by a responsible member of crew
7.9.4	Fire (special alarm to summon crew)	EM	AU	May be part of general emergency alarm
4.5.10.1.3	Hydrocarbon gas detection in tankers, cargo pump-rooms	A	AU, V	At the pump-room
+4.5.10.1.1	Temperature sensing devices for pumps installed in tankers, cargo pump-rooms	A	AU, V	At the pump control station
10.5.6.4	Fixed local application fire-extinguishing system activation	A	AU, V	In each protected space. Protected space is a machinery space where a fixed water-based local application fire-fighting system is installed
7.5.2, 7.5.3.1	Fire alarm	EM	AU	Audible alarm within the space where detectors are located
SOLAS III				
6.4.2	General emergency alarm	EM	AU	Throughout all the accommodation and normal crew working spaces
SFV Protocol 1993 Chapter II				
2(6)	Watertight door position	I	VI	At remote operating position II-1/13.6*
4(1)	Freezer room weathertight door position	A	AU, V	!, At the attended location
Chapter IV				
15(5)	Refrigerating machinery spaces alarm	A	AU, V	At an attended location (control station)
19(5)	Fire detection alarm	A	AU, V	At appropriate spaces when the ship is in harbour
20(1)	Bilge high water level alarm	A	AU, V	At places where continuous watch is maintained when navigation bridge is not manned II-1/35-1.2.6.2*

Table 10.1.6 – *Location: miscellaneous* (continued)

IMO instrument	Function	Priority	Display	Notes
SFV Protocol 1993 *Chapter V*				
14(2)(b)	Fire detection or automatic sprinkler operation	A	AU, V	Alarm at location easily accessible to crew at all times
15(2)(b)	Fire detection alarm	A	AU, V	Alarm at location easily accessible to crew at all times II-2/7.9.1*
Resolution MSC.128(75), annex				
4.1.2.4, 5.2.4	BNWAS second stage audible alarm	A	AU	Locations of the master, officers and further crew members capable of taking corrective action
4.1.2.5, 5.2.4	BNWAS third stage audible alarm	A	AU	Locations of the master, officers and further crew members capable of taking corrective action. If provided (ref. 4.1.2.6 of resolution MSC.128(75), annex)
SFV Protocol 1993 *Chapter VIII*				
2(1)	General emergency alarm	EM	AU	Throughout all the accommodation and normal crew working spaces III/6.4.2*
Nuclear Ships Code				
3.9.3	Spaces containing nuclear steam supply system safety equipment fire detection alarm	A	AU, V	!, Alarm at main control position and emergency control position
6.4.3	Controlled areas indication of radiation levels and airborne contamination	I	VI	At main control position
6.10.2	Containment structure purge system radioactivity alarm	A	AU, V	At main control position
6.10.4	Controlled and supervised areas exhaust for radioactivity alarm	A	AU, V	At main control position
2000 HSC Code				
4.2.1	General emergency alarm	EM	AU	Clearly audible throughout all the accommodation and normal spaces and open decks 8.2.2.2 of the 2000 HSC Code III/6.4.2*
7.7.1.1.4	Fire detection signal	A	AU	Clearly audible throughout the crew accommodation and service spaces
7.7.1.1.6	Fire detection manually operated call point section unit indicator	A	AU, V	Alarm at location easily accessible to crew at all times

Table 10.1.6 – *Location: miscellaneous* (continued)

IMO instrument	Function	Priority	Display	Notes
2009 MODU Code				
3.6.2	Watertight boundary valve position indicator	I	VI	At the remote control station
4.4.2	Oil-fired boiler low water level, air supply failure or flame failure	A	AU, V	Alarm at an attended location II-1/32.2*
4.9.1	Presence of water indicator	I	VI	
4.12.12	Cable tension and speed and direction of wind	I	VI	At a manned station
4.14.3.1	Jacking system overload alarm, out-of-level alarm, rack phase differential alarm (when provided)	A	AU, V	At the jacking system control station
4.14.3.2.1	Inclination of the unit on two horizontal perpendicular axes	I	MI	At the jacking system control station
4.14.3.2.2	Power consumption or other indicators for lifting or lowering the legs, as applicable	I	MI	At the jacking system control station
4.14.3.2.3	Brake release status	I	VI	At the jacking system control station
6.3.1.1.3	Loss of ventilation	A	AU, V	At a manned station
6.3.1.2.3	Loss of ventilation	A	AU, V	At a manned station
6.3.1.3.3	Loss of ventilation overpressure	A	AU, V	At a manned station
8.7.1	Fault requiring attention	A	AU, V	Including 8.3.5.1, 8.4.1, 8.8.5 and 8.9 of the 2009 MODU Code II-1/51.1*
9.10.1	Fire detection system alarm	A	AU, V	At alarm location easily accessible to crew at all times
9.11.1, 9.12.1	Gas detection and alarm system	A	AU, V	!, Alarm at a location easily accessible to crew at all times
5.7.2	General emergency alarm	EM	AU	Clearly perceptible in all parts of the unit III/6.4.2*
13.5.1	Wind direction indicator	I	MI	It should be free from the effects of airflow disturbances caused by nearby objects or rotor downwash and be visible from a helicopter in flight or in a hover over the helideck
13.5.26	Status light	A	V	To be visible to the helicopter pilot from any direction of approach
13.6	Motion sensing system	I	MI	Display should be located at the aeromobile VHF radiotelephone station

Table 10.1.6 – *Location: miscellaneous* (continued)

IMO instrument	Function	Priority	Display	Notes
1995 Diving Code				
2.5.2	Compression chamber internal pressure	I	MI	At central control position
2.5.3	Diving bell external pressure	I	MI	Within the bell
2.9.3	Diving equipment fire detection alarm	A	AU, V	!, At an attended location other than the above
2.11.2	Compression chamber/diving bell parameters	I	MI	At central control position
2.11.3	Diving bell oxygen and CO_2 levels	I	MI	Within the bell
FSS Code				
8.2.5.2.1	Fire detection or automatic sprinkler operation	A	AU, V	Alarm at attended location other than navigation bridge and central fire control station
9.2.5.1.3	Fire detection alarm	A	AU, V	Alarm at location easily accessible to crew at all times
9.2.5.1.1	Fire detection alarm not receiving attention	EM	AU	Alarmed to crew; may be part of general emergency alarm
LSA Code				
7.2.1	General emergency alarm	EM	AU	Throughout the accommodation and normal crew working spaces

*   Cross-reference to SOLAS regulation.

!   No location specified in other IMO instruments. Location is recommended.

+   These alarms may be omitted if they are provided at the cargo control station.

Table 10.1.7 – *Location: cargo control station*

IMO instrument	Function	Priority	Display	Notes
SOLAS II-2				
+11.6.3.1	Cargo tank high-level alarm and gauging	A	AU, V MI	!, If required
+4.5.10.1.1	Temperature sensing devices for pumps installed in tankers cargo pump-rooms	A	AU, V	
4.5.10.1.3	Hydrocarbon gas detection in tankers, cargo pump-rooms	A	AU, V	
Gas or chemical codes				
IBC 8.2.3 BCH 2.13.1	High level of the liquid in any tank	A	AU, V	!, (2)
IBC 15.10.2 BCH 4.3.1(b)	Failure of mechanical ventilation system for maintaining low gas concentration in cargo tanks	A	AU, V	!, Sulphur liquid
IBC 15.19.2 BCH 4.14.3	Power failure on any system essential for safe loading	A	AU, V	!, (2)
IBC 15.19.6 BCH 4.14.1	High-level alarm, cargo tank	A	AU, V	!, (2)
IGC 13.2.1 GC 13.2.1	Cargo level	I	MI	(2)
IGC 13.4.1 GC 13.4.1	High and low pressure in cargo tank	A	MI AU, (V)	(2)
IGC 13.6.4,17.9 GC 13.6.4, 17.11	Gas detection equipment	A	AU, (V)	
IGC 17.18.4.4 GC 17.12.2(d)(iv)	Cargo high pressure, or high temperature at discharge of compressors	A	AU, V	(2), Methylacetylene-propadiene mixtures
GC 10.2.2	Shutdown of submerged cargo pumps	A	(AU, V)	
IGC 17.14.4.3 GC 17.12.5(d)(iii)	Gas detecting system monitoring chlorine concentration	A	AU, V	!, (3)
IGC 17.14.4.4 GC 17.12.5(d)(iv)	High pressure in cargo tanks (chlorine)	A	AU, (V)	!, (2)
IGC 13.3.1 GC 13.3.1	High liquid level in cargo tank	A	AU, V	!, (2)
IGC 13.5.1 GC 13.5.1	Cargo temperature	I	MI	!, (2)
IGC 13.5.2 GC 13.5.2	Hull or insulation temperature	I A	MI AU, (V)	!

Table 10.1.7 – *Location: cargo control station* (continued)

IMO instrument	Function	Priority	Display	Notes
Gas or chemical codes *(continued)*				
IGC 13.5.3￼ GC 13.5.3	Cargo tank temperature	I	MI	!, (2)
IGC 13.6.11￼ GC 13.6.11	Gas detection equipment	A	AU, V￼ MI	!, (3)
IGC 17.14.1.4￼ GC 17.12.5(a)(iv)	Gas detection after bursting disc for chlorine	A	(AU, V)￼ MI	!, (2)
IBC 15.7.10￼ BCH 4.5.10	High level of phosphorus	A	(AU, V)	!, (2)
IBC 15.19.7.2￼ BCH 4.14.2(b)	Overflow alarm	A	AU, V	!
IGC 5.2.1.7￼ GC 5.2.5(b)	Liquid cargo in the vent system	A	(AU, V)	!, (2)
IGC 8.4.2.1￼ GC 8.4.2(a)	Vacuum protection of cargo tanks	A	(AU, V)	!, (2)
IGC 9.5.2,￼ GC 9.5.2	Inert gas pressure monitoring	A	(AU, V)	!
IGS				
3.15.3.2.1	Effluent drain valve position indicator	I	VI	!
6.2	Tank pressure sensors	I	MI	!, If required
VEC systems				
2.5.2.3	Tank overflow alarm	A	AU, V	!, (2)
2.5.2.4	Signal for sequential shutdown of onshore pumps or valves or both and of the ship's valves	A	(AU, V)	!, (2)
2.5.2.5	Overflow alarm and shutdown signal	A	(AU, V)	At an attended location￼ !, (2)
2.5.2.6	Loss of power to the alarm system	A	(AU, V)	!, (2)
2.5.2.6	Tank level sensor electrical circuitry failure	A	(AU, V)	!, (2)
2.6.4	Main vapour collection line pressure	I	MI	!, (2) VEC is equipped, common to two or more tanks
2.6.4.1	High vapour pressure alarm	A	(AU, V)	!, (2) VEC is equipped, common to two or more tanks
2.6.4.2	Low vapour pressure alarm	A	(AU, V)	!, (2) VEC is equipped, common to two or more tanks

Table 10.1.7 – *Location: cargo control station* (continued)

IMO instrument	Function	Priority	Display	Notes
FSS Code				
15.2.4.2.1.1, 15.2.4.2.2	Inert gas pressure	I	MI	
15.2.4.2.1.2, 15.2.4.2.2	Inert gas O_2 content	I	MI	
15.2.4.3.3	Inert gas system:			
15.2.4.3.1.1	– low water pressure/flow	A	AU, V	
15.2.4.3.1.2	– high water level	A	AU, V	
15.2.4.3.1.3	– high gas temperature	A	AU, V	
15.2.4.3.1.4	– blower failure	A	AU, V	
15.2.4.3.1.5	– oxygen content	A	AU, V	
15.2.4.3.1.6	– power supply failure	A	AU, V	
15.2.4.3.1.7, 15.2.2.4.6	– water seal low level	A	AU, V	
15.2.4.3.1.8, 15.2.4.3.4	– low gas pressure	A	AU, V	
15.2.4.3.1.9	– high gas pressure	A	AU, V	
15.2.4.3.2	Gas generator failure:			
15.2.4.3.2.1	– low fuel supply	A	AU, V	
15.2.4.3.2.2	– power supply failure	A	AU, V	
15.2.4.3.2.3	– control power failure	A	AU, V	

!   No location specified in other IMO instruments. Location is recommended.

(2)
(3)   See notes following paragraph 10.2.

+   These alarms may be omitted if they are provided at the pump control.

Table 10.1.8 – *Location: not indicated by IMO instruments*

IMO instrument	Function	Priority	Display	Notes
SOLAS II-1				
5.6	Draught indicator	I	MI	Passenger ships only (if required). For details see regulation II-1/5.6 of SOLAS. Recommended location: wheelhouse
SOLAS II-2				
4.5.10.1.4	Pump-room bilge high-level alarm	A	AU, V	Recommended location: wheelhouse or engine control room
4.5.4.2	Flammable vapour monitoring	I	MI	
Gas or chemical codes				
IBC 7.1.5 BCH 2.15.5(a)	Alarm and monitoring of cargo temperature	A	A, V, MI	Alert system only required if overheating or overcooling could result in a dangerous condition Recommended location: wheelhouse or cargo control station
IBC 13.1.1 BCH 3.9	Cargo tank levels	I	MI	Recommended location: cargo control station
IBC 15.7.7 BCH 4.5.7	High temperature of phosphorus	A	AU, V	Recommended location: wheelhouse or cargo control station
2009 MODU Code				
4.10.15	Draught indicator	I	MI	At an attended location II-1/5.6*

*   Cross-reference to SOLAS regulation.

Table 10.1.9 – *Location: central ballast control station of column-stabilized MODUs*

IMO instrument	Function	Priority	Type	Notes
2009 MODU Code				
3.6.5.1	Watertight doors and hatch cover position indicator	A, I	V, VI	
3.6.5.2	Watertight doors and hatch cover position alarm	A	AU, V	
4.9.8.1	Flooding detector	I	VI	
4.9.8.3	Propulsion room and pump-room bilge high water level alarm	A	AU, V	
4.10.10.2	Ballast pump status-indicating system	I	VI	For details see also 4.9.12 of the 2009 MODU Code
4.10.10.4	Ballast valve position-indicating system	I	VI	For details see also 4.9.17 of the 2009 MODU Code
4.10.10.5	Tank level indicating system	I	VI	For details see also 4.9.14 of the 2009 MODU Code
4.10.10.6	Draught indicating system	I	VI	For details see also 4.9.15 of the 2009 MODU Code
4.10.10.7	Heel and trim indicators	I	VI	
4.10.10.8	Main and emergency power available indication	I	VI	
4.10.10.9	Ballast system hydraulic/ pneumatic pressure-indicating system	I	VI	
4.10.14.1	Ballast tanks liquid level	I	MI	
4.10.14.2	Other tanks liquid level	I	MI	
4.10.17	Ballast valve position	I	VI	!

! No location specified in other IMO instruments. Location is recommended.

49

11   References

11.1   *IBC Code.* International Code for the Construction and Equipment of Ships Carrying Dangerous Chemicals in Bulk (resolution MSC.4(48), as amended).

11.2   *BCH Code.* Code for the Construction and Equipment of Ships Carrying Dangerous Chemicals in Bulk (resolution MSC.9(53), as amended).

11.3   *IGC Code.* International Code for the Construction and Equipment of Ships Carrying Liquefied Gases in Bulk (resolution MSC.5(48), as amended).

11.4   *Gas Carrier (GC) Code.* Code for the Construction and Equipment of Ships Carrying Liquefied Gases in Bulk (resolution A.328(IX), as amended).

11.5   *SFV Protocol 1993.* Torremolinos Protocol of 1993 relating to the Torremolinos International Convention for the Safety of Fishing Vessels, 1977.

11.6   *IGS.* Guidelines for inert gas systems (MSC/Circ.282, as amended by MSC/Circ.353 and MSC/Circ.387).

11.7   *2000 HSC Code.* International Code of Safety for High-Speed Craft, 2000 (resolution MSC.97(73), as amended).

11.8   *VEC Systems.* Standards for vapour emission control systems (MSC/Circ.585).

11.9   *IMDG Code.* International Maritime Dangerous Goods Code (resolution MSC.122(75), as amended).

11.10   *1995 Diving Code.* Code of Safety for Diving Systems, 1995 (resolution A.831(19), as amended).

11.11   *2009 MODU Code.* Code for the Construction and Equipment of Mobile Offshore Drilling Units, 2009 (resolution A.1023(26)).

11.12   *Nuclear Ships Code.* Code of Safety for Nuclear Merchant Ships (resolution A.491(XII)).

11.13   *FSS Code.* International Code for Fire Safety Systems (resolution MSC.98(73), as amended).

11.14   *LSA Code.* International Life-Saving Appliance (LSA) Code (resolution MSC.48(66), as amended).

11.15   *Resolution MSC.128(75).* Performance standards for a bridge navigational watch alarm system (BNWAS).

Appendix

Sample of indicator columns with dimensions (mm)

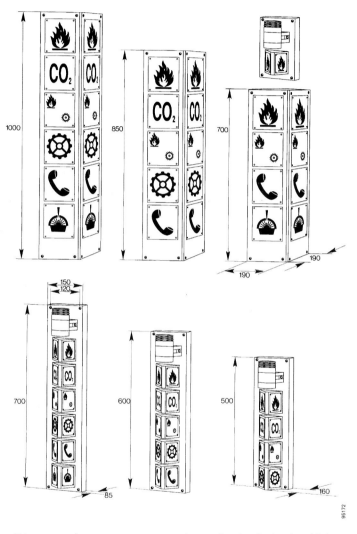

Note: Diagrams above are representative only. Symbols should be as in tables 7.1.1 to 7.1.3.

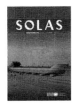

SOLAS Amendments 2008 and 2009

This publication presents amendments to the SOLAS Convention concerning, in part:

- emergency towing on tankers (chapter II-1)
- the 2008 IS Code (chapter II-1)
- protection of vehicle, special category and ro-ro spaces (chapter II-2)
- passenger ships safety (chapter II-2)
- the IMSBC Code (chapters II-2, VI and VII)
- bridge navigational watch alarm system (BNWAS) and electronic chart display and information system (ECDIS) (chapter V)
- the Casualty Investigation Code (chapter XI-1)

Language	Sales No.	ISBN
Arabic	I175A	978-92-801-5000-1
Chinese	I175C	978-92-801-6078-9
English	I175E	978-92-801-1520-8
French	I175F	978-92-801-2435-4
Russian	I175R	978-92-801-4000-2
Spanish	I175S	978-92-801-0202-4

Life-Saving Appliances, 2010 Edition

This publication contains the three most important IMO instruments dealing with life-saving appliances, namely the International Life-Saving Appliance (LSA) Code, the Revised Recommendation on Testing of Life-Saving Appliances and the Code of Practice for Evaluation, Testing and Acceptance of Prototype Novel Life-Saving Appliances.

Amendments adopted since the previous edition address, amongst others:

- stowage, fitting and equipment of liferafts
- certification and fitting of lifeboats
- new requirements for fast rescue boats
- requirements for lifeboat and rescue boat launching appliances
- carrying capacity of free-fall lifeboats
- changes in the average weight of persons to be used for the design and equipment of life-saving appliances
- extensive new requirements for lifejackets, including the introduction of infant and child lifejackets

Language	Sales No.	ISBN
English	ID982E	978-92-801-1507-9
French	ID982F	978-92-801-2389-0
Spanish	ID982S	978-92-801-0174-4

Visit www.imo.org for your local distributor

4 Albert Embankment • London SE1 7SR • United Kingdom
Tel: +44 (0)20 7735 7611 • Fax: +44 (0)20 7587 3241
Email: sales@imo.org
www.imo.org

INTERNATIONAL MARITIME ORGANIZATION

PUBLISHING

Notes

Notes

Notes

Notes

Notes